Shastra Deo was born in Fiji, raised in Melbourne, and lives in Brisbane. She holds a Bachelor of Creative Arts in Writing and English Literature, First Class Honours and a University Medal in Creative Writing, a Master of Arts in Writing, Editing and Publishing, and a Doctor of Philosophy in Creative Writing from The University of Queensland. Her first book, *The Agonist* (UQP 2017), won the 2016 Arts Queensland Thomas Shapcott Poetry Prize and the 2018 Australian Literature Society Gold Medal.

T0340778

Shastra **Deo**

The Exclusion Zone

UQP

First published 2023 by University of Queensland Press
PO Box 6042, St Lucia, Queensland 4067 Australia

University of Queensland Press (UQP) acknowledges the Traditional Owners and
their custodianship of the lands on which UQP operates. We pay our respects to their
Ancestors and their descendants, who continue cultural and spiritual connections to
Country. We recognise their valuable contributions to Australian and global society.

uqp.com.au
reception@uqp.com.au

Cover design by Sandy Cull, www.sandycull.com
Author photograph by Kate Lund
Typeset in 11.5/14 pt Adobe Garamond Pro by Post Pre-press Group, Brisbane
Printed in Australia by McPherson's Printing Group

 **Queensland Government** University of Queensland Press is supported by the
Queensland Government through Arts Queensland.

  University of Queensland Press is assisted
by the Australian Government through the
Australia Council, its arts funding and
advisory body.

Excerpt from *Living Myths: How Myth Gives Meaning to Human Experience* by
J.F. Bierlein, copyright © 1999 by J.F. Bierlein. Used by permission of Ballantine
Books, an imprint of Random House, a division of Penguin Random House LLC.
All rights reserved.

A catalogue record for this book is available from the National Library of Australia.

ISBN 978 0 7022 6551 8 (pbk)
ISBN 978 0 7022 6672 0 (epdf)

University of Queensland Press uses papers that are natural, renewable and recyclable
products made from wood grown in well-managed forests and other controlled sources.
The logging and manufacturing processes conform to the environmental regulations of
the country of origin.

 **MIX** Paper | Supporting responsible forestry FSC® C001695

The urge to self-annihilate occasionally overwhelms the best of us. Exhibit A: the atom bomb. Exhibit B: love.

—Laird Barron, 'Gamma'

All a poet can do today is warn.

—Wilfred Owen, 'Preface'

CONTENTS

THE EXCLUSION ZONE

THE GAME ROOM

THE LIGHTHOUSE

THE EXCLUSION ZONE

You are searching for something.
You have searched for a very long time.
You have crossed the length of this land and back on
your hands and knees.
You wait for someone to answer.

Turn to page 5.

Fukushima Soil

For most of my life I've been right
about omens. Salt, ravens. Red skies at morning.
Rocks thrown against the wind. A six
-pack ring found in the vicinity of a sparrow's nest
suggests three loves before marriage. A robin's egg: split
ends. Stones skipped over an oil-slicked lake are lucky, luckier
still by an evening bonfire, flame
licking the corner of a clamshell
punnet of strawberries. To be born
on uranium-rich soil is to say something about granite, sunflowers,
polymer. The transfiguration of telluric into human
object. A prophecy is only as good as its seer, and no witness
is ever on time.

Today I was divining the melt point of a bulk bag:
the heat required to spur an entanglement of matter, amalgam
of polypropylene and Fukushima soil. The time it takes to write
radiance into rock. What remains
after passing is plastiglomerate, pressure, and the cascade
that rots caesium to barium. What departs is various.
It was many years ago, now, when a stone was just a stone.

You don't remember this place. This land could be
arid or hungry or wet or rot. That does not matter. Your memory
can't tell you what no longer exists.
This is what is certain: something is here
and it wants to hurt your fleshy body.
Stone spires erupt from the earth, frozen yet
emanating like objects in motion, tall as
trees, taller, much taller.

Do you remember trees?
They crowd you. Show you how it feels to be small.

You came here because this landscape of thorns
blocked your view of the horizon.
You stay here because you don't yet understand
this wounding.

To investigate the spires, turn to page 71.
To go further, turn to page 63.
To go home, turn to page 89.

Canto for Sumitomo Bank (Hiroshima Branch)

It was only after the
end that I could see new ways of seeing. No apparition
or soft ghostling, but then nothing of me had left yet. None of
              me was gone. I wished often for these:
an easement of lead, a funeral mask to the faces
of my earthy becoming. The worms. Roaches. Little moulds in
              their minor rottings. In the
    all-night I believed I alone emitted light within the crowd,
throng of us feeding the straight-snaked necks of sunflowers, petals
        rich with us. As if we weren't also musing on
hunger. As if an entire roaming of life were not committing a
      witness of my bruiseless body: gleaming, wet
at my bent elbows, one human shadow cast in stone, like a black
        -bird   on a bone-white bough.

Pavlovsk Station

Protoplasm is in perpetual motion. Even with speakers silent
the drum of booted feet, bare feet, staccato spilling to shuffle softness
keeps us living. The mother plants still breed true. We're not so
different from the Fragaria, it seems: both craving milder days,
quiet nights. Among Rosaceae unrimed it's easy
to forget the famine. Siege
-song on my tongue to keep from swallowing leaves. Science
has yet to prove it, but we know berries grow better
with light, water, and the strains of a gardener's
tune. Someone will remember this refrain had two parts.
Twenty years from now, a student of Saint Francis will learn the
value of our days. In California fifty years on, Phocas
reborn will speak of mothers and their
daughters, how they dig up the mothers,
dig up the daughters, how they'll throw away the mothers and
send him the daughters; Fiacre, perhaps, will turn
away, and Dorothy will weep.
I know no other hymns. There are many saints here.
And soon, too, martyrs.

Post-detonation Linguistics

Fact: things are like other things. Supposition: liking
tweets is like a simile. A house on fire. Like
an inconsequence. My love
is like a rose. A daikon radish. Birdsong
like a car alarm. My love is like
a transuranic element. Or a glass half full
of milk five minutes
from the refrigerator, suspended
between palm, floor,
and the condensation that coats it.
Fact: some things are something
else. A thought is a single
-celled organism. Supposition: to speak
is a rhizome. My
love is a vowel sound. An assonance. A
round mouth's red. Fact: the poet tells
me my bones are already ninety
per cent cold
-war detritus, which is to say
the act of telling bears the fact, not
the bones. Fact:
a prophet is always a poet, but not the reverse. A prophet
is an apocalypse. An apocalypse a sheet
pulled off a rear-view mirror. A moment's
sun is days, minutes, or millirems. Accumulation
a spending. My love
is a spatial category. A semiotic
decomposition. A childhood is a Kodak film
canister, or

a raw-boned calf
muscle in white knee
socks. My love is
a poet. My love is the face of a poet really, which
is the face of the hunter half
transformed into stag or wounded
dog. A doe is a laurel tree. My
love is a baseball bat. My love is a wound
-up clock spring, a temporal dissonance, a metaphor
is conceit, my love is like my beloved is
the species of dark
and warmth that closes over
hands in coat pockets in
an air-conditioned room.

You've lost the word arctic but you know all about masses on masses of sun-damp snow.

To go back, turn to page 23.

How Deep

we actually buried it remains
a secret, though in advance
of an accident we created
signs, songs. The poem

remains a secret. Though time
grew heavy, our bodies
created signs, songs,
the poem: our wasting language.

Time grows heavy. Our
bodies could not be
forgiven. Our wasting
language, the depth of this

silence, could not be forgiven
in advance of the accident. We,
the depth of our silence. How
deep? We buried it.

Aubade (Earth-TRN688)

Some miles from the border they heave up
the remains of the body that tried to run
them off the long road home. The boy
nudges the jellied mess of an eyeball
with the toe of his boot.
POISON, the other says.
LIKE THE BLACK RAIN IN ARIZONA.
it's very cold out, says the boy, thinking of the
eye in its orbit
on the tongue. No-one is watching.
He dips his finger into his mouth and picks
at the flesh caught in the ridges of his molar.
HUNGRY
the other says. Sucks saliva from their gums.

—

The only thing that grows from the soil is a contusion
the colour of chewed plums. Dark and viscid
as the other in the depths of his throat. The white
day. Sky stippled pink like the smooth
muscle of the stomach.
Then stones in a stream that stopped.
THE PAST IS ONLY INFORMATION
ACCUMULATED OVER THE BREADTH OF ONE LIFETIME
they say. YOU DO NOT NEED IT
TO KNOW WE EXIST.
The old road it churns beneath the new road.
And like any person porous and monstered

by all things that move through the world
they get used to it.

—

where is home. WHERE YOUR SUN SETS
where is home. HERE eddied in the intercostals, the breathing
      room of the chest
where is home. HOME IS YOU
where LISTEN TO YOURSELF

—

Lungs. Liver. Pancreatic
juice. Intestinal bacteria worn
thin by the white day's exhalation.
The boy tells them of a king who
devoured himself to end his famine.
The other sniffs, trails over the tight
scaffolding of his ribs.

—

On the fortieth day the boy's thyroid begins to turn
so the other decides
to eat it.
He tastes like a river in spring. Inside is a pearl
that pops to tar warm
as a live rabbit. They chew thoughtfully,
leak a sliver of themself into the boy's mouth and grasp
his trachea, tender as a wound.
LIKE THE BUTTERFLIES, they try, IN THE STOMACH.

The boy, inexplicably, begins to cry.

—

It is not that the other
has gouged a white space within him in which
only they can fit. But who else will tooth his sinews, lick
the sweat at the musculature of his back,
swallow the dermography
of time that seeks to line his skin. Who in any wasteland
would not eat around the shape of their better self.
Any love can be heavy
as a handsaw held teeth down to a thigh.

—

After a hunger inside them so raw he retches
handful after handful of petrified
wood, they say, TELL ME A STORY. The boy
bites the skin at the base of his left thumb. *once,
there was a boy and he was loved
in a way he couldn't understand.*
ONCE THERE WAS A BOY AND HE WAS LOVED ONLY
WHEN HE WAS USEFUL. *once, like all boys*
a boy hid a cat in a box weighed with an old hammer.
He did this only so he could be the one
to help it return home AND YOU
SHORED THAT ROILING MEMORY AGAINST
THE CURVE OF YOUR LUMBAR SPINE
where the other reaches for it
like an oil slick spilling into the red wet
of a shark carcass.

i don't remember that. I DO.
I WILL REMEMBER IT FOR YOU. I DO.
They spend the night there
remapping axons and dendrites
reading him.

—

Somewhere between the
first of the red days he loses the
word for stone.

—

something wrong THERE IS NOTHING WRONG *wrong*
     inside of me YOU ARE IMAGINING THIS *i don't remember*
  TELL ME WHEN YOU SEE YOUR SUN
          SET *i* WILL REMEMBER FOR YOU *let me*
 go LISTEN TO YOURSELF *please* [   ] *darling* [   ] *please*
                   NO

—

What they have learnt is the surest archive is a body able
to shed the slough and organs of itself in order
to become that much more of the world. How
many pieces of him are moth and pitch and the viscosity that swirls
at his sternum. What of the bile they left in Colorado. Memory
bone-white in the raw flesh of his jaw. That past
is futureless. His skin
the only nation.

—

THE TERRIBLE THING ABOUT YOU, the boy swallows,

IS THAT I THINK YOU ARE NO LONGER HERE

—

hungry, the boy says. The other
says nothing, crouched
on their heels towards the wind
as though listening for a
longing
transmitted from great distance.
To the west is a coast is
one hundred and sixty days of salt. The boy
makes it audible to them.
An edible present. A biological winter.
When he leaves, they think
they will know this land exists.

—

They hold the boy in their body until the bright red dawn.

Things We Inscribed in the Voyager Golden Record

A calibration circle. A concept. Addition and calculus. The sun. Its light spectrum. The light. Black-body radiation. Refraction of light in a riverbed. A god of fishermen. The amber current encasing three brook trout. A vermiculate pattern. Anatomy 1 (the skeleton of a trout in shallow water). Anatomy 2 (internal organs front). Anatomy 5 (rib cage). Schematics of the eye. Liver. Pancreas. A bone (lacrimal). The DNA structure of a Fukushima barn swallow. A Fukushima barn swallow. A rapatronic photograph taken within ten nanoseconds of nuclear detonation. A picture of a nest. A picture implying that the things that preceded it were not merely representations but objects occupying space and time. Time. Radiophobia. A family portrait. An apotropaic poem. A pine tree. A memory in its becoming. The spoor of him in June (bergamot, ginger, tonic). An ecological education. Cicada song that outlives summer. An empty carton of Seven Stars. Apartment interior with brother and firearms. A home. A hole. A cellar door. An X-ray of his abdomen from 1986. An echo. The half-life of fear. A house being constructed. A man in construction. Sotenbori River and the same river at night. Early morning test light. A dog and its bark. Fifty-five greetings. Fifty-six elegies. The Brandenburg Concerto No. 2 in F Major. 24-hour Cinderella. Instructions for dancing. Instructions for waking up. A single-use plastic slipper. A softshell turtle (*Trionyx japonicus*). Fishing line taut as his jaw. *Disiecti membra poetae*. A trauma diagrammed from start to finish. An exit sign. Underwater scene with captor and exit wound. An exit.

You are surrounded by message. Something is trying,
very hard, to be told.

यह स्थान रेडियोएक्टिव कचरे के लिए एक दफन स्थान है। हम
आपको बताने जा रहे हैं की नीचे क्या है, आपको इस जगह को परेशान
नहीं करना चाहिए और यदि आप करते हैं तो क्या हो सकता है।
आपको यह जानकारी देकर, हम चाहते हैं कि आप अपने और आने
वाली पीढ़ियों को इस बर्बादी के खतरों से बचाएं।
कचरे को नमक की परत में दबा दिया जाता है। नमक को चुना गया था
क्योंकि इसमें बहुत कम पानी होता है और कचरे के अवशेष के लिए
कमरों को खोदने के कारण दरारें होती हैं। कचरे के नीचे दबावयुक्त
खारे पानी की एक स्थान होती है। सतह के नीचे एक चट्टान की परत
होती है जो स्थान बनाते समय पीने योग्य पानी नहीं होती थी।

The text goes on, and on, and on. In the time it takes for
you to read it, entire languages go extinct.
This must mean something.
It must mean.
It must.

To go back, turn to page 23.

Frameshift Mutations

she did not ask you for jaw and lip
you foe yet kin for era
but you awe the men who ate her
raw roe gut doe eye wet
god his maw and pax was bad for her
nix the rib but you are not her ilk

she can not ask him for jaw and lip
her foe yet kin for era
but hea wes the men who ate her
raw rob gut elk eye dry
god His paw was pox was bad for her
saw the leg but hei sno the ril k

hec ann ota skh imf orj awa ndl ip
zhe rfo eye tki nfo rer a
uth eaw est hem enw hoa teh er
xra wro bgu tel key edr y
god _is was pox was for her
awt hel egb uth eis not her ilk

Poem for My Son in the Years of a Hot War

Know I lived through a time when my dreams were more
than this: a *good morning* at morning,
sleep well at night. Rough-hewn
slice of rye before dawn. A story
told honestly. Laundry, fresh-folded,
in the almost-dusk light. I am young
enough to know certain qualities of light can pass
through the cells of the skin, the soft

tissue of a boy's body, moving
like a blaze through brittle forest. To dream you
in the bleach light of a dirty
bomb detonated outside the bakery
two blocks down, night-sun
kindling your limbs like signal fire.
Body the panorama of a man
-made sacrifice zone. But that comes later.
There are ledges in time on which it is safe yet
to stand still. Every day

it is morning. Every day I throw back the curtains and
watch you turn towards me like a listening
ear. Watch you breathe
the dust of ten decades. Watch you pull
away, sleep-soft, your body
carrying your body, as though
you don't yet know the weight
of those that you love.

Every day the wash of light
over bedcovers. Your hand. Your
cheek. Your eyelid, lifting.

Corporeal Needs Questionnaire

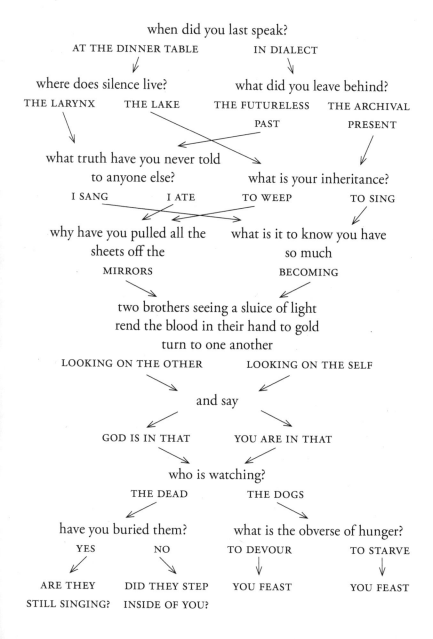

when did you last speak?

AT THE DINNER TABLE   IN DIALECT

where does silence live?   what did you leave behind?

THE LARYNX   THE LAKE   THE FUTURELESS   THE ARCHIVAL

PAST   PRESENT

what truth have you never told
to anyone else?   what is your inheritance?

I SANG   I ATE   TO WEEP   TO SING

why have you pulled all the   what is it to know you have
sheets off the   so much

MIRRORS   BECOMING

two brothers seeing a sluice of light
rend the blood in their hand to gold
turn to one another

LOOKING ON THE OTHER   LOOKING ON THE SELF

and say

GOD IS IN THAT   YOU ARE IN THAT

who is watching?

THE DEAD   THE DOGS

have you buried them?   what is the obverse of hunger?

YES   NO   TO DEVOUR   TO STARVE

ARE THEY   DID THEY STEP   YOU FEAST   YOU FEAST
STILL SINGING?   INSIDE OF YOU?

It's quiet inside, yes, but you hear a distant hum.
It's not enough to make you turn back. Not yet.
You've walked far enough with the weight
of a wasteland on your shoulders. We have carried
forward the knowledge
that everything, even history, slips through our hands.
How long will you spend here, chasing ghosts?
Do you understand what it is you're doing here?
A long corridor stretches out before you. On either side of
    you, doors.
You sense that you can go deeper.

अपने बाईं ओर का दरवाजा खोलने के लिए, 18 पर जाएं
अपने दाईं ओर का दरवाजा खोलने के लिए, 27 पर जाएं
सीधे जाने के लिए, 10 पर जाएं
नीचे जाने के लिए, 48 की ओर मुड़ें
To go back, turn to page 89.

Baby Tooth Survey

for Jini Maxwell

I.
they age us by our fall
teeth: we were born

long after the fissure. hairline lilt of sea
lichen, a mouth full
of benthic parnassus. our bicuspids said

the shoreline, though sheltered,
was not enough to keep us clean.

2.
millstone in marrow, sponge
-soft, cumbers to sarcoma. its half-life exceeds
our expectancy.

bone seeker,
you never told me
exactly what science took from us.

3.
someone strips dental consonants
from our first language. someone culls
our syntax to extinction. we

cut eyeteeth on dead coral, amanita gills. your sleight
of tongue trips, treads
empty alcove of my speech.

4.
your name incised in wrist of deciduous reef. this is where
they buried them, once-traded: twice

-traded they will turn to gold. this
is where your bones lay

against my bones.

View of the Sky from an Imagined Lake in June

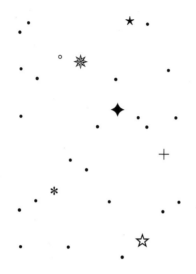

★   Let's say we read starstuff the same way we read bait minnows in a mesh net: like punctuation flitting over a metrical foot, or a lake limned with stones, liminal space, soy sauce fish.

°   Sometimes you have to hold a thing to understand what to do with it. How it governs you. How the scrimshaw of our beloved bodies bends too far back. Skin grown over splinters & chemical peel. Mistakes between the faultfissures of our fingers.

✻   How often does belly grow heavy with / remarkable error! / bezoar wrought of slough, cinders and capital? How often is a heart just like a fish in the hand?

✦   Pulsing / still / pulsing.

+   Let's say we read starstuff the same way we read calculus. Which is to say, // I can't.

*   Sometimes holding a minnow in your teeth means it congeals into matter that drives diaphragm & breath. Sometimes you swallow the fish in your hand and it's just plastic and shit.

☆   'I don't appreciate,' my mother / says, 'that sort of language.'

, sun

To go back, turn to page 23.

Interlude (Creek Mouth)

far from the lure that opens the meltwater
a trout yawns
around a gambol of tadpoles
the belly the brook the one
last holding place
in these days when all things
are only what they are

Undertakers of the Atom

for Madeleine Dale

And so we buried them in our trenches, those old
soldiers who burnt without flame, that
wood, its earthbound root we broke, brick

-bark warm to the hand as a live rabbit.
When I held the death I was sure
I could not kill it in any way that mattered. What I mean

to say is if living is a matter of matter
being arranged in a particular way
then yes, okay, alright

they're not quite living. But dig up a Chernobyl pine
and you'll see an incorruptible saint, a myroblyte
body, the weight of its air writing itself into the cells

behind the eye. This is not war, yet
the isotopes of peace are longer lived
than those of the bomb.

What I will know for certain a quarter
of a century from now is this: there is
birdsong. There are swans skimming the cooling

pond and catfish at depth. Unbury a Chernobyl pine tree
and you will find a rabbit by its trunk-wound still
as a fallen peach.

What I mean to say is here
you must forget a thing to kill it.

What I meant to say was everything

oh

everything lives.

Przewalski's Horses Are Back in Belarus

the last wild stallions have stabled themselves
at the border

look at them
striding between the couch grass
as they nip at the bumblebees

their round white bellies full
as a hungry child's or a mare foaling
more horses into the world
than there lived that morning

those miracle machines
powered by the same
strontium that warps blood and marrow

by the birches
the birds' nests
in cottages rotting against
the clouds

powered
by the knowledge that people
were never needed here at all

Irish Book of Spells

Once, three sorceresses of Maeve were roasting a dog over
a fire, and Cuchulain broke one geis to keep another

—J.F. Bierlein

Geis wherein the poet's every memory features an apple tree.
Geis wherein all memories of apple trees are replaced by apple
        trees perceived through windows.
Geis wherein the poet dreams over one thousand three hundred
        and fifty times a year.
Wherein the poet can never again stand by a window.
Know that the poem is not about heroes.
That the poet may not gaze upon the bomb.
The poet carries language through international waters, will
        never find the right words to quantify the extent
        of their exposure to ionising radiation.
The poet cannot write about spring.
Geis wherein sunflowers only signify sunflowers.
Geis wherein the warning is always a riddle.
And the poet's teeth seem for laughing round an apple, the poet
        who will live until the world ends, and those who did not
        have to die will watch with their eyes fixed on the last
        point of a horizon unsaid by an idle tongue.
Geis wherein the dead are watching.
Geis wherein the poet may not kill birds.
Geis wherein people fall in love twice. The poet will fall in love
        five times,
          if they're lucky.
The poet is not permitted to write about love, or poetry.
The poet is recognised only at dawn. Can only prophesy the past.
Geis wherein an elegy may be to the next.

Wherein the poet is a dark star in the orbit where the lover once
       blazed, and the poet may look anywhere but the sky.

The wound seeks out the arrow.

The war must be silent.

Geis wherein the true poet must be truthful.

Geis wherein the poet must be saved, if the letter of the poem
       would last, if the spirit of it
       survives …

Geis wherein nothing happens: not war, not song.

We will all be forgiven.

Walkthrough

Find a centuries-old oak. To walk there will be slow work. Listen.
Kill three wolves. There will always be wolves.
Kill the man who wears a wolf pelt on his back.
Enter the cave mouth and follow the flooded dirt path.
Reach a mass of heart roiling within roots. Do not
touch it. You were told not to touch it. You were told what
  you should do.
Remember. See yourself moving but not what moves you.
   Far past the hillock in a village called Downwarren a
   woman may hand you a fist of white myrtle under the
   light of an old seer's moon.
Eat them, or brew, with celandine and sweet alcohol, an
   antidote to pops' mould. You may
take the woman to bed but none would advise it. You may
repay her with a wolf's liver but none would advise it.
Travel south by morning.
Gather one raven feather and a spirit's buried bones. You
   were told where to go. You are not wanted here or
   any place along the long road.
Remember that you are the monster and a monstrosity must be
   read.
Keep walking. There will be black horses. There
   will be fields of black horses rippling through
   breeze. There will be a moment when you can
make the right choice.

THE GAME ROOM

Transcript of a Fight Scene
Between Several Yakuza at the South End of Iwao Bridge

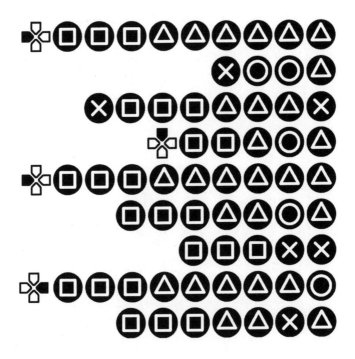

I'm no new game fool. The algorithm tends towards strength,
statistics, men who still search for you   men
who are never going to leave you alone. So you can go
    wherever you want and do whatever you want to do, but baby,
                    who'd live like this on purpose?
What the fuck ever. This is a fight scene. Chin down, batter up,
dance like we want to win. Show me how you bruise and I'll
        show you how to run from this. How
    the body fails to let go of the body. Tonight you're thinking
you're thinking   I'm thinking there's nowhere left to go,
    I'm thinking what now, what then? If this is the gap
between omen and event, if then, what now, and then, and then
    when are we? I could mark time by the woman waiting
                for us in the dark of a locked
warehouse while she feels her way out with her hands. Time
                by contusion, grovel in inverse, a caught sparrow's
        last bow of flight. By getting under your clothes. If your
skin still looks like the translucent casing
            of a wireless DUALSHOCK® 4 controller,
guts on show, that means we're lucky. If you're swallowing
    down the blood in your mouth, that means we're finally
making sense. Humour me:
                what are we doing with this body?
        The depth of this relationship is currently limited
    by the machine. The border between us isn't so clear.
So what! So you want me to say I'm sorry, so
                sorry, you want me
to ask you where it hurts, where in this place does it hurt,
    where, when, when are you, when does it hurt? This is a fight
    scene. Take out the guy with the knife; we didn't tell him
                he could get inside of us, and nothing kills

morale like getting felt up for nothing.

    Somewhere in the dark a woman is waiting for us to take her
       hand with the hunger of a history that has not yet
    happened. I won't be the one to tell you
      what's already passed. Let me take it back.
This is a fight scene. Okay. So a bite to the throat is a bite
  to the throat, but a tongue on the teethmarks says, *this is play.*
  So a bat to the face is a bat to the face, but my hands
    on the controller say, *this*
is play.   Here is the part where I get my money's worth,
inhabit the loading screen between nowhere and not here, here is
    the path between cutscene and event. Drop the post-game
       swagger: I know how this ends. A body exists
only to verify our own existence. You're thinking of yourself in the
    first person singular as though we're not one
      of those snakes that survived by eating our own heart.
    I'm looking for someone
        to take you home. Knit the pink fascia,
restless meat of your jaw. Spit-shine your baseball bat and you'll
spit up a thank you. Will you dance like this forever?
      I take it back. The algorithm tends towards
freedom, but the flow of information doesn't always go both ways.
  Listen, baby,
     come to bed.
      I can't tell you a story that doesn't already exist.

Self-portrait as Goro Majima

I like trying on your body. Tilt of your hips, thew and sinew, swivel
the right stick to see how
you look on me: wrung out, worn thin. Brittle grin of you stretching
us into fists. Your smart mouth's
red. How you can't stop naming yourself. How in a foregone
future you
bare your taut belly as though the bodies of these men aren't set
to ruin us. As though the rind
of your knees can keep the blood inside of you. They couldn't
render your scars so instead we hold
a closed eyelid, empty socket, hair absent on your fine-boned wrists.
You already carry
a woman on your back. What's one more?

I want a change
of skin. We haven't yet been married, but you're a family man.
Hands just like a father's. Press
× to interact. Press ○ to cancel. Reverse the trajectory of this
body, the throatful of sham
dialect and smoke. Spit oozing back into you. Swell of you fits
better than I ever did. I don't
know where you've been, but I could take us
to karaoke, and drinks, and
tripe barbecue, swallow your snake's tongue, wet pillow
of your chest. Forget that
you were ever anything less than powerful, insides of our thighs
marking the year
when no-one came to save us. Tap ×
repeatedly to surface. Hold × to dash. You can only

sprint for so long. I don't have the currency
to help you outrun this.

I'm not controlling. You can idle as long as I let you: smoke, ash,
smoke and stretch, roll the breadth of our knotted
shoulders, shudder
and breath. Press □. Press □. Press
□. Animal whimper, Δ and chokehold, a lover's tight
clench. Have you noticed our body's
all wrong? Remember
when we could keep both eyes open? Flash back to April,
before I could move you, when I could only
pause or turn away, watermelon
we smashed to pieces, our hand and its gesture towards the last
days of spring, the sticky
-hot joy of you before we knew
exactly
what we would do to each other.

Fishing at Caer a'Muirehen
for my brother

I forgot to say noon was closing around us. Further
up the mountain, fog spills thick as curdled milk
but here the air is cool. Cedared. You are pulling your
shirt away from your skin, building breeze, fabric pinched
in your fingers. Your bucket heavier than ours combined.
The youngest of us, a bomb fisher, holds his tongue
in his teeth as he threads his hook. You don't see.
You are watching for bears, perhaps, or calculating
the hours of light left by the weight of our three shadows.
Politely ignoring the sweat smell trapped in the soil
at the backs of our knees. The sweet smell of blood
crusted in your hairline, just behind your right ear. How
long had it been since someone saw you? You flinch,
reel in that writhing muscle, scale tinged pink as the
flush on your nose. I no longer need you to like me.
We can't know it yet, but on the eve of our father's
passing some years beyond the past, each one of us
will learn that only a brother, no matter his goodness,
sees you as god sees you. Only the youngest of us
would debate the difference between boys lost and stolen.
Sorry. I'm not telling it right. I was minding my line. I
am minding my line as our brother declaims the value of
controlled detonations, his voice louder and louder
on each outbreath, your laugh catching on the second of
softness in your belly. I know every lie you've told
about earthworms and perch. This is what the world, in these
centuries away from you, has taught me: no fisherman
can become a good man. No one of us will die
in our beds. When it comes I am begging you to
be what buries me.

Can you trust yourself not to come back here? Remember
that old incantation

> *new mexico*
> *nevada*
> *onkalo*
> *bure*

in the voice of your ancestors?

Do your children still sing
to their children after dark?

I wrote you this song because memory collapses time.

I wrote you this song because I knew you'd outgrow me.

Turn to page 89.

Don't Look Down

By thirteen I could leap atop the garden wall
on my own two feet. I liked to best in the afternoons
when the sunlight was rich as a peach, my father still
in his meditations. I had skinned my knees three times.
Never under the gaze of his cat eyes, but that mattered little
when he would staunch the bleeding, beds of his fingernails red
and red. He found me once, one foot balanced
against the stone, one foot pointing towards the dust motes
and the light. The quiver in my leg clear in the air.
Don't look down, my father said, standing
in a patch of fool's parsley, his arms outstretched
as though to stop the promise of scab, his arms wielding
the same hands that carried my things and my treasures and
my hands. But I looked. To see him I looked.

The Break

The first time my daughter broke her ankle
the air was thick with rain. I didn't hear her
shriek because she didn't, trusting my body
to weather her body and carry her inside.
I twisted the hem of her trousers to her calf,
hands predicting the bruise, the shape of
her minutes from now, made too small for her skin.
Then I fetched ice and a towel and roughed her
hair until her breath was mostly laughter.
I think I opened my mouth then, and shut it,
my jaw closing with that click she liked and
imitated, teeth chattering with none of the cold.
I had wanted to say that no-one did this for me.
That it is impossible for us to live without
pushing beyond a safe range of motion. But
you are biting your words, she said, and, before I
could swallow, pushed her porky little fingers
right past my lips, feeling for my incisors.
She remembers this to me often, but forgets
the next morning: the girl creaking all throughout
the kitchen, breath solid as a gannet's wing.
Boiling eggs, setting spoons out, sweet rasp of
her voice as she saw me in the door. Crutches
thumping against the stone tile. She poured
tea into my cup and pressed it, bowl-first,
into the unexpected cradle of
my hands, her smile easy as she let go, weight
listing towards the strong half of her body.

The Act

The doe doesn't care. Has never seen
a deer leap highest. If these are hunters
they bring empty hands.

At this distance she can't see which
is the shadow of the other. Doe and the man. Or doe
and the girl. Caught in the act of seeing.

The shadow turns and strips a limb
of its branches, walks five steps, looks back
at what cast it. Quiet among the cedar legs,

the doe and the darkness, each of them
looking at one certain thing and
thinking, this is mine, mine

alone.

The Hanging On

First day. My father tracking one axis
deer. Tomorrow morning a fallow.
Come evening I'll make fire and char
the meat for eating. My hands are good
at that now. Turning one thing to another.
I want to describe how once
this was the only place I could be what
I was but today what I want is to
go wherever my daughter is, in the years now
when the sun freckles her arms and dirt
cakes her fingernails. But that's a feeling
I don't have nouns for. I was the same age
when I watched my father take an axe to
the fox with a paw in the foot trap. The sound
that left it frightening rabbits from their warrens.

You've heard the phrase 'hot cell' once before.
Someone has told you the centre of all things is warm
as a live rabbit clutched in the hand.
I have yet to disprove these four premises:

> That you are curious.
> That you become safe through burial.
> That you become dangerous again through your naming.
> That too often we seek our own disposal.

There's nothing else here. All I can hope
is that you believe me.

> रहने के लिए, 53 की ओर मुड़ें
> To leave, turn to page 43.

Learning a Dead Language

In my twenty-fourth year my father
makes me tea for the very first time.

He is between brewings, made three tinctures
for the son of the man due

west of here, to ease the belly
and the dreams. I wait for him to read

my fortune. Next is buckthorn and ribleaf
for a mother who travels five days

to see him, bryonia for a gardener
wishing for rain.

He has started growing his own bison grass.
Winter cherries in window boxes

which he shows me with shyness and pride.
I go too long between these visits.

I have never been good with eventualities.
He examines my cup. Fiddles

with the deer heart in a bowl by his hand.
He stands to make me another

scooping the mess out with his fingers
at the roots of the orange trees.

Interlude (River Causeway)

a day when the fish
can be taken
for granted
alone at the
river mouth as black
rain gluts
land to marsh
wet in the marrow
praying without knowing
to what
wondering if the fish
does the same
now
at the end of the line

Something Ends

This is the first time I see him
    in profile. The brush of his arm against mine in the cold.
      He is a careful man, my father. Steering us alongside our
footprints as though it were that easy to delineate time and space.
     Then, he walked beside me. Now, he walks beside me. Proof of it
    captured in snow on snow.

We break the lake ice and catch four fish for dinner.
    We collapse in the sleet clearing under the weight of our
      laughter. No matter the winter we shed long shadows, mine
encased in the cast of his lonely body. For once
    we have not come so far that there is nowhere
      left to go. But he, on the verge of my leaving, says

tell me

    about the time you held the hand
                 mirror, how it was
      spring, and you had climbed up the parapet, refracting
   catches of sun to strike my temple, and before you
                 I would have been a decade's
      length across the continent but there under the lintel
      I would have given the meat of my own leg for our
silhouettes to remain dreamless and changeless and mindless
    of survival, and that you
       know, you must know, the most loving
        words I could give you were knowledge

and he looks at me as a father looks at anything, knowing
    that this was too good to live for long.

        I tell him. I leave
    nothing out. There is time, still, until
we must go back.

Perhaps you still don't understand what this place is.
Perhaps you do not care. Outside of here is the agony, the
life. It's too easy to get trapped in the past.
But it's warm here.

I wrote you this message because memory collapses time.

I wrote you this message because I hoped you'd try again.

Turn to page 89.

Orichalcum

I don't know what will happen to my body
afterwards, but I want to return
to the reservoir outside our home town
where we caught catfish in the summer,
my father close to kneeling
at my feet. The tender press of his thumb
against the skin beneath my eye, the tear
there. Clumsy fingers cradling the curve
of my skull. The catfish thrashed in his free hand
and I did not realise the reach of the sunlight
was critical.

The last time I saw him, my father stood
as he stood in the brook-bed: tall like the Victory
of Samothrace, ruin braced
in the shadow of his back. In the water I looked at him
as we look at the things we've lost:
the crag of his brow, smile mapped clear
in the crook of his cheek. Cartographies
of silence. The way he sank down
as if struck. The catfish, violent
with panic in the naked air.
Alive and gold.

The Question of an Ethical Shot

you left the body in the mountains.
no incense for your brother, no burial.
goneness of him clean and hot. the body

was not his, nor was it yours

to take: gutshot, frenzy,
spilt intestines rime-crisp. cheek frozen
to frost earth. no meat wasted, come spring.

this is not an escape
so much as a mourning
of such tender want.

—

where to shoot deer: close
to clearings, beds, food plots;
away from deep rivers, ice; away
from home. where

to shoot deer: the neck,
heart
-lung, high
in the shoulder, snap spine and shock the nervous
system, keel
to anchor.

—

butchers require a steady hand,
soft touch, and

your hands have not committed
softness
for a long time.

—

the heart-lung is forgiving. haemorrhage easy
to find and follow. you know
how he sounded
when struck in the ribs, the throat. when

he hungered. moments before
sleep, rangy
muscle of him hanging
from the crook of an elbow. your mottled
boyhood and all its grace.

what is a body
whose only trace
is silence?

—

where to shoot bears: brain, neck,
shoulder, lung.

a bear's heart is often protected

by its upper leg.
avoid the abdomen, unless aiming
to track or torture. the soft part of the belly
is best for eating.

—

your brother had no softness
to his belly
but the bullet still stuck.

a gutshot animal will inevitably go to water.

—

snowfall gnaws raw into cubital fossa. pithed
for a bruising. what
is a body to a butcher's hand? meat

to tongue?
you haven't stopped
chewing, which is to say

your living

no longer feels like betrayal.

—

you leave your body on the mountain.

no incense, no rage. sometimes
a border is marked only by passing
through again and again.

you could kill a man to become him but this
has already happened.

this is not an escape

but maybe the end of it: the last
of the ice under your cheek
            thawing out.

THE LIGHTHOUSE

Galatea Wakes Six Feet from Ground Zero

after Kaitlin Wadley's 'Blood from the Stone'

it is easier to want
after nightfall: being
     of your being born
     in blood spill, shedding
          all that light. what blueprint sits
               unfinished in you, your
               body the wound
          between object and eye, architecture of your
               brain built brimful with memory
     that sits seen but unseeing. the space
          you fill and the space that fills you
is a muscled expanse, and so little
     of the universe is empty.
          you can't cut deep enough to hit bone, but
               skin is its own story.   inter:
pushing soul into body is
     violence and I will not forget
          to bleed. in your godhood you
       dis-
         mantle and
           re-   member
     what comes back, what
     sleeps under stone until the mourning
          cloak is lifted, what excavated absence
opens its eyes in the dark and stirs.

On the Proper Disposal of Limbs

Bury it. Mark it
with stones arranged
like the constellation of Virgo.

Pelops has no place
in night skies;
defer to Demeter

instead. Incineration
is popular but I want to be able
to find it again.

Formalin preserves;
keep it on the mantle
or send for cleaning

and articulation. The latter, and
no-one can know
where the flesh goes.

Bury it. I want it whole
when I light candles and stand
for séance, step and stagger five

feet like that doomed
surgeon-soldier, join hands
with the sisters, and go

dancing.

You find your way to a pillar carved with symbols, delicate
as onion skin, leaking mania.

खतरा
जहरीला रेडियोएक्टिव कचरा यहां दफन हो गया
यहां खुदाई या ड्रिल न करें

A question: can you read it?
Another: do you know what it means
to read?
Here it is necessary to believe that the act of reading is a part of
something bigger.
There is still time to turn back.

To go further, turn to page 86.
To go back, turn to page 89.

Shastra Deo

I have no middle name. My mother did
not deign to pay homage to relatives
or ancestors, though I was given the bridge
between my aunt's first and married names.

शास्त्रा, Shastra, may refer to a treatise,
to sacred scripture, yet it's almost always
a suffix, equivalent to the English *-ology*:
meaningless unless attached to a subject

of perceived value. I have no Hindu gods to speak
of, no kinship with Dharmashastras, but
I know Apollo: his plague, poetry and prophecy;
Bragi and his cupful of promise. I can no longer

pronounce my own name. An inexperienced tongue
makes a trochee of me, where instead one should
hear stressed feet: a spondee, second syllable
far from plosive, *t* pronounced with the tongue

at the tip of the teeth, like the *thrall* in thraldom.
In Old High German Deo means servant, yet
despite the fall of Rome we return to gods many
-minded and duplicitous, god as object. *Deo* the dative

and ablative singular of *deus*: deity. देव is
perhaps a variant of the Sanskrit *Deva*: divine,
godlike, masculine. But Deo is a last name
of Demeter, so claimed by Orphic Hymn,

most likely derived from the Cretan δηά:
dea. I am not adept at harvest, not mistress
of a grain labyrinth: I have killed a lemon tree
and suppressed my own eggs. Still, Demeter

presides over sacred law: a goddess of divine
order, treatise and scripture unwritten.
Were my names reversed, *Deoshastra*, I
imagine it would be easier to speak

within my skin, recite the *Devas* with my paper-filled
mouth. Instead I am morpheme, foregoing
divinity: my name stripped of accents and spun
on a flat tongue, foreign gods clenched

in one small fist.

Sorry

I haven't yet scaled the fish for dinner, I was caught
up in picking the lemons to slide under the skin, which one
should probably do when the skin is more skin than scale,
but what can I say? You can never pick too many lemons.
I'm sorry I forgot to record the first ten minutes
of the 5 pm quiz show that started while you
were walking the dog, I know you like it, and the dog, I'm
sorry I do not labour over the intricacies of dogs, I find
more to love about horses, though I fear them, too, but
it is better to both fear and love, I think, so thank
goodness I am feeling both for you right now! I'm sorry
I didn't hear you come in, I was distracted by the state
of the kitchen, which admittedly was my doing to begin with
when I cleaned out the cutlery drawer searching
for the juicer, the scaler with the wood handle, I see now
that the can opener would have been rather useful
for the dog food, or the tinned peaches we could have
eaten in syrup and evaporated milk, which I much
prefer to the canned fruit salad with the grapes that are
not quite tough enough on the tooth, I'm sorry, I know
you like how those grapes give way when you press your
tongue to the roof of your mouth, like a
grape, I suppose, under a carriage wheel, or underfoot. But I
have always admired the tension a fresh grape's skin maintains
over its flesh, like the skin of a horse's lower leg: horse
legs having barely any subcutaneous tissue, that proud
flesh and alright! I'm sorry for the horses. Most of all
I am sorry you'll have to wake up beside me when
again I may be talking about horses as you watch

the shadow of our lemon tree sway as it
paints itself on the wall above my head, sorry for
you, not myself, who all in all has come out of this life quite
lucky, I'm sorry to be thinking about horses while you think
about the lemons, if there are enough left for two tall glasses of
lemonade for us to drink in the pink afternoon, but
you should check the fridge, perhaps, and I will maybe have
the good sense to tell you I am sorry
I thought of that first.

Grey Walk from Carseldine Station, September 2020

The sky gestures towards rain. Mountains
a smudge in the west. By the soot
brick fencing a series of townhouses
named Hillside Manor, a magpie darts
to the drain grating and back. I knew her
two springs ago, before the lichen
brightened the wild quince trees. She knows
what it is to be a daughter.

From the heights of a weathered wood telephone
pole, her children beg for her. Remembering
in the tilt of her head, nape of her neck
proud, glossed grey. Were I a romantic
I'd claim she gleams in the sunset. But
there is not enough light
for that. She claps her beak, once. Sings
what I am called
and watches me go.

A Short Future of Deluge

Fed by rainwater run-off, melted hailstones, and water from punctured single-use plastic bottles, the Kohaku River formed in 1988 and to this day is home to various species of catfish, bitterling, and minnow. Fishing was lush until 1995, when a near-drowning spurred local officials to fence off its swift waters. A 1996 land reclamation project saw the River drained and replaced with quick-set cement: the foundation for a block of apartments few asked for and many bought. In the following years, apartment residents complained of leaky taps, unforeseen water damage, and laundry that was impossible to air-dry. For a single moment on a summer evening in 2001, the glass of every interior apartment window was covered in condensation that had the same taste as tears. Little changed over the next decade, but, by the end of the century, rising sea levels resulted in mass flooding and the restoration of the Kohaku River, whose amber current teemed once again with the living and the dead. Many ask if the River can truly be called the River; its new waters trace back to the polar ice caps, and its bed is now composed of footpath and apartment detritus. But most agree that it is impractical to talk about the water when one is really talking about the River, that a river, flowing with new water, is still, nonetheless, the River. Despite the lack of human habitation, visitors to the area often report seeing what looks like a lone cherry salmon reeling upstream; on closer inspection, the object is always revealed to be a child's bright-pink shoe.

Interlude (Reservoir)

the fisherman
unsinking
a sealed capsule of caesium salt
unhooks his catch and
throws it back, throws
it back

Few things speak anymore but the spires
tell you that you are not welcome. That you should be ready
for a bruising.
The stone is weathered by the patina of passing hands.
Someone has been here before, in another life, in another time.

To climb, turn to page 77.
To go further, turn to page 63.
To go home, turn to page 89.

How to Love Like a Horse
after Mindy Gill's 'A Kind of Paradise'

What I know about desire is horses
who aren't hungry can't be owned
by anyone. The horse, she bows to no-one
well, she bows
only for bribe, wheedle and charm, only
for a patch of fresh clover, or an apple to chomp
to pieces. A horse is a good thing to think on
when I can't speak neatly. Our jaws
working in tandem. And maybe she bows
to carry you from there to where
-ever the earth allows us to walk
to my fetlocks, knowing
that to love is to sometimes keep
one's feet off the ground,
and to look on a horizon is to see only
the past. A horse is a good place to be,
strategically. And here I am understanding
that horses know to wait
for their happiness: the swing of a muzzle
into the chest of her beloved, a hand muscling in
at the withers. That big horse heart at rest.
Eating the clover at dusk, knowing
the next day will be twice
as lucky.

The Task of Shooting Me

I know little of the ways
of hunters: what offerings
you'd bare for a dendritic
crown, your hand to hot
flank, a hoof full of sound.

I have only ever been caught
in the crosshairs of birdsong.

Your spine may be spindle
and tether for the wants on
your teeth, but the laceration
on my furred belly
can cut cord to the quick

and dead. You will soon forget
me and my pine-lichen cloak.

I am not a body to be bridled.
This is not a field brimming
with burn enough
to scorch the carcass clean.
You can't contain hunger

by chewing on bone, lest you find
a taste for phosphorus.

While Making Love with a Combat Medic

Stitch our disunion into the gutshot
split my belly, suture. Spare me
your hand and bandage. Kneel:

your thighs bracket my hips
as you etymologise me. Body
of my father in the skin

around my eyes. Night-bathed
I want no light but stars and fire.
Bloodletter, you only take me

after dark. Needle your semantics
into my sartorius, trace the muscle
the morphology, with your mouth.

What tender masonry you build
in my limbs. Carve your decree
in milk light, mark me

with sweet relief. Doctor and polemic
you craft me: a lexicon of want
awaiting your translation.

Lilac and Gooseberries

I love you as a sister lures her younger sister to the
cottage where the younger sister's husband waits
out the full moon because he is a werewolf. Surprise!
It ends badly. The husband devours his wife and
wakes the next morning, innocent, memoryless,
wondering where his love has gone. And his
sister-in-law cries both for her guilt and for her
love that is hungry enough to eat a woman whole.
So I love you as that sister-in-law loves: all-wanting,
unconditionally, in a way that ends badly, like an
animal loves another animal when fucking or eating
or any other synonym for the same thing. Which is
trite, probably. But so is the crescent moon overhead,
and the cedar trees, and you casting the window
open before bed because storms gift you the scent
of wet stone. I think of you as that stone
thinks of itself as a cast-iron skillet when under
the sun at noon, body black with soot that a
spymaster scrapes to make ink, write letters, which is
to say I love you as a letter hunts its recipient across
enemy lines, as a widow greets newlyweds
over her dead's bread and salt, or an old woman stews
apples in a frying pan she thought was lost. As children
play war I am walking past the apple trees as
though all paths and trees would lead near to you,
or to lilacs, one of which is true, past the corpse
eaters, the orchards, the wolves the rabbits run from, I
love you as that hare there, caught below the bramble,
still bending its neck to bite the gooseberries.

Bone Nest

My hands can recall the memory
of your hands, the holding

as familiar as the turn
of a doorknob, a kitchen knife

clenched in a fist. When I wither,
you'll find someone new to run

fingers over the framework
of your ribs, cradle your calcaneus,

read your liver and scrimshaw
with twinned palms, my coiling

tendons gone soft, wingspan of
my phalanx bones woven

to hold little birds in their nests.

No nests here.
There is a legend that says human history was hidden
in the shell of a sparrow's egg, but all your prophets
have forgotten how to read
the birds. From here
you can see the thorns radiate, fill an entire expanse.
From here you can pretend that you are separate from this.

To climb down and go further, turn to page 63.
To leave, turn to page 89.

Curse Poem

You will catch diphtheria.
You will find a dead woman's bones.
You will save a man and he will kill four others.
Your little horse, a chestnut mare, will spook at the sight of blue.
Your next meal will be cold. And the one after that.
And the one after that.
Every twelve days the seam in the armpit of
your favourite shirt will come loose.
You will find a pebble in your shoe.
You will gather five wolves' livers and anger a woodland spirit.
You will travel from town to town but fail to set roots.
When you sneeze you will sneeze in fours.
You will be too early or too late.
You will drink with your daughter.
You will forget her birthday. She will tell you a story and
you will not let her finish it.
She will walk heart-first into a season of frost thinking
you thought nothing of her.
You will go to bed thirsty.
You will find a necklace lost long ago but have no-one to give it to.
Here's the thing: once this ends
you will wake in the silence of your childhood home, sweat at
your neck and between your thighs.
Your hair will grow thick at the roots. Your posture enviable.
Your mother once left you by the side of the long road and
you will know, given the choice, she would do it again.
You will live here alone. The
weather will be as it always was and
you will plant verbena and honeysuckle and green-scented

lilies. Your flowers will flourish. All will live in
spite of frost and insects and the desire to give too much
love. It will rain, and it will rain when rain is needed most.
You will be caught in a hailstorm. A relict beast
will trample your garden, knock its horns against your side.
Lie still a moment. One more.
You will live here. You'll be good at this. Soon
you will reseed your seedlings.
Eat six grapes and close your eyes as you
tongue the textures between skin and flesh.
Fingers pressed to the hurt yet to bruise.
The air will clear.
You will have to pay taxes.
You will listen so hard
you'll hear a dandelion seed float
overhead.

Search History[1]

We had forgotten how to imagine other worlds.

—James Bradley

I tell this story in the conditional: we may have known
the future. We may have done nothing. The space
between us might have been lush as the understory you lacked
language for. So I tell this story not with language but with
the flight path of a forest wren as it cuts through
breath and thought and knowing and air. Knowing
that maybe once we ate the days away
like a summer's peach
when we still lived by the seasons, the juice dripping right
down to the wrist
the elbow. The bend of our bodies calling back, perhaps
to our ancestors.[2] And yet
I am still searching for the self[3] that I am.

—

1 how to be beautiful
          how to be beautiful overnight
          how to speak
          how to speak well and listen better
          how to listen to trees
          noun for listening to a twig break
          verb for eve
          adjective for evening

2 RealLifeLore 2016, *Are You Related to Neanderthals?*, online video, 5 November,
   YouTube, <www.youtube.com/watch?v=AoRsa0Q5pA0>.

3 Marris, E 2018, 'Neanderthal Artists Made Oldest-Known Cave Paintings',
   Nature News, Nature Publishing Group, 22 February, <www.nature.com/articles/
   d41586-018-02357-8>.

In this time gum trees bend under the weight
of cyclone winds. You are still
here. You are in the next room.
Yet I remember you more
than anything
as our house seen from a distance
of twenty paces along the drive
the windows lit up
in the days all houses in lonely forests
looked like little ships circumventing their way
through the night.

—

Some mothers have forgotten what it is
to be a daughter.

—

I have seen pictures of the brain, but
I do not believe them. I believe in spring.
Storms. Lightning
that lumbers through the skull, nerve
branches flooded: light right down
to the root.

I believe in endings. I believe in the shape
of your hand[4] as it curves
at my cheek. And I know it.

4   You know where to find me: earth.google.com/web/@-
     43.04761699,146.63158783,915.55877315a,9558.24023814d,
     35y,-0h,0t,0r

I know, also, a great many things I do not believe.

—

Wild lilies are growing everywhere you stood now, same
colour as the shadow you showed
me on the scan
the night our home dropped anchor on the first break
of light.

—

Perhaps I am asking for space.

                    Perhaps I am insisting we see space

          and its silence

                        as the only way back.

—

I may have learnt this with you in the garden,[5] though
I learn it now, again and again: the growth from seed
to sprout to seed
is like one kind of love
becoming another.

What do the trees think the world is made of?
What do they read in our messy biology, hospice

---

5   The Guild of Ambience 2017, *Forest Sounds | Woodland Ambience, Bird Song*,
    online video, 6 April, YouTube, <www.youtube.com/watch?v=xNN7iTA57jM>.

that feeds each roam of roots? Have they refigured
you to leaf or wildflower or
limb? So I tell this story as
though they still think of us
in this time
and all the times before and after
the after:

You may know it's coming. That does not make it easier. or:
Your shore and my own will be of different worlds. or:
I love you.
or: Sometimes a shoreline stretches so far there is nowhere left to go.
and: I'm sorry. and:

The sea only keeps you
as long as the journey allows.

—

If you plot this search on a map[6] it looks like a
wave washing across the
world, the trajectory by
which we become
ancestors.

—

The story of matter is this: nothing dies.
Patterns of information, electricity
and biochemicals, deep web of nerve and neuron, limb

6   www.google.com/maps/d/u/0/
    embed?mid=1fTNry-KHzYjRAA15GifL1npXIIna4Qky

and stem, remake to microbe and geosmin. Leaf litter
of an ever-season. Smell of soil after rain. The
matter of matter is this: nothing
is storyless, not even the dead.

The knowledge of matter is this: you are gone from me.
You will never again raise your hand to shade your eyes
from the low light. Feel for fever
with your palm pressed to my cheek. Here
you must forget a thing to truly kill it.

And yes, we are forgetting.

—

So I am remembering to imagine another world.
History runs backwards. An ending
by which to begin. Unstuck from time
the story goes like this:
matter arranges itself in the movement of the living.
Mud glistens as river flood resculpts the roots of trees,
ice rain so full of sea it aches with it. Fish spit
hooks out past their lips and little
birds suck their songs from the air. Silence
loud as an echo. And in this
rebecoming I return home to you. The lightning
that racks your brain recedes, years

wash off you like salt from a wound. And
I hold you as if I were the mother and you were the
alchemy that conjures north through the needle
in my mind's quiet eye, and I hold you until you are so

small the world cannot ask you to carry its weight,
and I hold you until you change everything and nothing.
The waters sink and rise and flood and flood away, the
blackfish thrash in the streams in the mountains, and
by the geography of a once-remembered world my
careful body bears me to the self that I am, and I can
tell you that I know, I love you, I'm
sorry, I know, and the key, the word, the story is

—

if I am telling you this then I
then there is nothing I would not give or do or leave behind
then in the long years I will hear the stories of the birds
and the fish and the whales and the dolphins, I will hear
them in the witnessing of each arc
of flight, of torque required to twist fin through earth
if I am telling you this then
I am a story still going
then we are a story still going
and there is still time, and there
is still you
and if I am doing the telling then
I will begin the story here, and it begins like this:

yes
there is a way forward
though there may not be a way back

You can't turn back. The longer you stay
the more you believe this is a place destroyed,
not built. Before you
a wall, another etching:

इस जगह को इस खतरनाक सामग्री को लोगों से दूर रखने के लिए
चुना गया था। इस क्षेत्र में चट्टान और पानी असामान्य नहीं लग सकता
है या गंध नहीं हो सकता है लेकिन रेडियोएक्टिव कचरे से जहर हो
सकता है। जब रेडियोएक्टिव पदार्थ का क्षय होता है, तो यह अदृश्य
ऊर्जा को बंद कर देता है जो लोगों और जानवरों और पौधों को नष्ट या
नुकसान पहुंचा सकती है।
इस मार्कर को नष्ट न करें। इस अंकन प्रणाली को पिछले दस हजार
वर्षों के लिए डिज़ाइन किया गया है। यदि मार्कर को पढ़ना मुश्किल
है, तो लंबे समय तक चलने वाली सामग्रियों में नए मार्कर जोड़ें और
उन पर अपनी भाषा में इस संदेश को कॉपी करें।...

Consider the hands that wrote this message. What
they looked like. If they looked like yours.
If they were displaced by time into rain and breath.
If the heart that drove them echoes.
In the distance you see a structure, enclosed;
it reaches out to you, pulsing with promise.
Are you afraid? You can still leave. I was afraid, once.

आगे जाने के लिए, 23 की ओर मुड़ें
To go back, turn to page 89.

The Light's Winning
for Paul Taucher

listen, man, here's the thing, the thing is
I'm tired, the drive's long, the turn's
sharp, my hands at six and nine
on the wheel, and I know
I've never been to Alaska but god knows I trust
Siri more than your jacked-up faded memory
of a town, and I know everything
we've done or ever will do will happen again
and again and again, it's 4:20 am and I'm tired, man, tired,
and I don't need you
to tell me what's poetic about death and time and
meat, to tell me it's easy
to spend too long getting good at bad things, tell me
about the monster at the end of each
story, about death not being
the end of it, about
our children
and how they wait for us
despite the cosmic indifference
of family homes, hospital rooms,
of the long bright dark
before sleep.

Lychee Season

Like any person during spring I am
standing outside the house as the sun sets.
My neighbour's windows bloom with the lean light

of afternoon, the bees dawdling still
in the wattle. A magpie sighs on the chill perch
of a satellite dish. To my left the road

carries cars to or from home
and a man shouts through an open window, maybe
saying, *hey beautiful*
or saying just for the pleasure
of saying. So

like any person watching the dark
eat up the day I am, despite everything,
believing I live in the beginning of a better world.

And the clouds, as if in answer, doing
what they were born to, ease open
for the fresh-peeled moon.

There is nothing I wouldn't give to try again.

Notes

The choose-your-own-adventure poem 'It Survives' simulates exploring the Waste Isolation Pilot Plant in the far future. Engaging with ideas from the field of nuclear semiotics—which posits, in part, that language will degrade faster than radioactive waste, highlighting the difficulty of communicating with far-future generations—this poem is also partly written in Hindi, a language that was lost to me over one generation alone. Curious reader-players can use the 'camera' function of an app like Google Translate to delve deeper into the text.

'Fukushima Soil' borrows and alters sentences from Roland Barthes's essay on plastic in *Mythologies* and Anne Carson's poem 'Short Talk on the Withness of the Body'.

'Canto for Sumitomo Bank (Hiroshima Branch)' takes the last words of each of its lines from Ezra Pound's poem 'In a Station of the Metro'.

'Pavlovsk Station' is an elegy for the scientists who starved to death while protecting the gene bank's edible plants, seeds, and tubers during the siege of Leningrad.

'Post-detonation Linguistics' borrows and alters lines from Wilfred Owen's poem fragment 'I Saw His Round Mouth's Crimson' and e. e. cummings's poem 'if there are any heavens'.

'Aubade (Earth-TRN688)': Earth-TRN688 is a Temporary Reality Number in the Marvel Database and refers to the branch of reality in which the film *Venom* (2018) occurs.

'Baby Tooth Survey' is loosely inspired by the St Louis Baby Tooth Survey, during which researchers studied children's deciduous teeth to determine the health effects of nuclear fallout on human anatomy.

'Irish Book of Spells' borrows and alters fragments from Wilfred Owen's poems and unfinished preface.

'Transcript of a Fight Scene' borrows fragments of Goro Majima's dialogue from the videogame *Yakuza 0*.

'Self-portrait as Goro Majima': Goro Majima (真島 吾朗) is a recurring character in the *Yakuza* videogame series.

'Fishing at Caer a'Muirehen', 'Don't Look Down', 'The Break', and 'Something Ends' respond to the videogame *The Witcher 3: Wild Hunt*.

'The Act' reworks the first line of Emily Dickinson's poem '[A wounded deer leaps highest]'.

'Orichalcum' responds to the videogame *Final Fantasy XV*.

'The Question of an Ethical Shot' is a response to the 'Hunter and Killer' side-story in the videogame *Yakuza 5*, as recounted to me by Jini Maxwell.

'On the Proper Disposal of Limbs' responds to Silas Weir

Mitchell's American Civil War–era short story 'The Case of George Dedlow'. When the story was first published anonymously in the *Atlantic Monthly* in 1866, many readers assumed it was an autobiography written by its narrator: soldier, assistant-surgeon, and quadruple amputee George Dedlow.

'Shastra Deo' is after Bronwyn Lea's poem 'Bronwyn Lea'.

The title 'How to Love Like a Horse' is after Ada Limón's 'How to Triumph Like a Girl'.

'Lilac and Gooseberries' was written for Yennefer of Vengerberg (*The Witcher 3: Wild Hunt*) and borrows its structure from Kenneth Koch's poem 'To You'.

'Search History' responds to James Bradley's novel *Ghost Species*. It was originally commissioned by Brisbane Writers Festival for their 2020 showcase *Room to Dream*. The digital iteration of the piece can be explored here: padlet.com/shastradeo/searchhistory.

Acknowledgements

This book was written on the stolen lands of the Jagera and Turrbal people. Always was, always will be. I acknowledge the ongoing harm that nuclear weapons testing and uranium mining are inflicting on Aboriginal communities; I acknowledge the ongoing resistance and resilience of First Nations people in the face of colonial violence.

Thank you to the editors and staff of the publications where poems collected here have previously appeared, some in earlier forms or under different titles: *Antithesis Journal*; *Any Saturday, 2021, Running Westward: Newcastle Poetry Prize Anthology 2021*; *Australian Poetry Journal*; *Best of Australian Poems 2021*; *Brisbane Writers Festival: Room to Dream*; *Cordite Poetry Review*; *Going Down Swinging*; *Ibis House*; *Island*; *the lickety-split*; *The Lifted Brow*; *Liminal*; *Meanjin*; *Overland*; *Peril*; *Running Dog*; *Scum Mag*; *Shuffle: An anthology of microlit* (Spineless Wonders, 2019); *Southerly*; *Stilts Journal*; *TERSE. Journal*; *Tincture Journal*; *Verity La*; *The Weekend Australian*; *WellBeing WILD*; *Westerly Magazine*; and *Wildness*.

Thank you to the judges of the 2020 Tom Collins Poetry Prize and The Moth Poetry Prize 2020 for commending 'The Break' and 'Fishing at Caer a'Muirehen' respectively.

Thank you to Jessica Wilkinson and Quinn Eades for your valued advice on this manuscript in its early stages.

Thank you to Maria Takolander for your keen eye, kindness, and generative conversations; to Aviva Tuffield for your persistence, patience, and warmth; and to Felicity Dunning for your meticulous feedback and unwavering support.

Thank you to James Bradley, Bella Li, and Sara Saleh for your thoughtful readings, and for your generosity.

Thank you to Laird Barron for allowing your words to be the entryway, and to Wilfred Owen for being truthful.

Thank you to Bronwyn Lea, without whom this book could not exist.

Thank you to Rosie Clarke for bearing the lantern.

To my brother, mother, and father—thank you, thank you, thank you. Thank you. You already know which of these poems are about you.